Original title:
Solar Flair

Copyright © 2025 Creative Arts Management OÜ
All rights reserved.

Author: William Hawthorne
ISBN HARDBACK: 978-1-80567-779-6
ISBN PAPERBACK: 978-1-80567-900-4

Mysteries Glowing in Orbit

In a dance with quirky stars,
Hopping around in cosmic bars.
Jupiter's winks, Saturn's laughs,
While Pluto just takes silly selfies for crafts.

Asteroids roll like bowling balls,
Comets slip on spacey shawls.
Galactic pranks that twist and twine,
The universe just chills with a glass of wine.

Chasing the Cosmic Embrace

A rocket sneezed, and off it flew,
Chasing a cloud, it made a goo.
Stars giggled 'til they turned bright red,
While aliens barked like dogs in bed.

A meteor shower, what a tease,
Dancing on the galactic breeze.
Cosmic creatures in joyful trance,
Swirling in a starry dance.

The Ember's Lullaby

The sun hums softly, a golden tune,
Holding hands with the giggling moon.
Fireflies join with a twinkle and shake,
While tiny suns play tag, make no mistake.

Chasing shadows, the stars spin round,
A symphony of laughter in the night found.
Comets showcasing their wild ballet,
In this merry game, we'll forever stay.

The Glinting Path of the Day

Through beams of light, we skip and play,
On a pathway made of bright sunray.
Sunscreen on, we sizzle in glee,
While laughter echoes from tree to tree.

The flowers wave with petal charms,
Inviting the sun into their arms.
Every shadow tells a funny tale,
In this bright world, we cannot fail.

Against the Twilight Sky

In twilight's glow, it seems absurd,
Giant marshmallows, fluffy and blurred.
They float up high, like they're on a spree,
Who knew clouds could host such a zany decree?

A jester sun, with a wink and a roar,
Dancing in circles, who could ask for more?
It tickles the horizon, though it's just a trick,
A cosmic laugh that makes time feel quick.

Celestial Fireworks

Stars pop like corn in a midnight strut,
Comets are sparklers, and boy, what a gut!
Planets don party hats, all twinkling bright,
They'd dance if they could, such a whimsical sight.

The sky is a canvas where laughter will bloom,
With giggles from Venus, and Mars in a costume.
A festival up there, but nobody knows,
They just think it's stardust, that sparkles and glows.

The Warmth Beneath the Surface

Underneath the crust, it's toasty and bright,
Fossils exchanging jokes in the night.
They burble and chuckle in their rocky domain,
Like old pals reminiscing while playing a game.

Down below, it sizzles like bacon in a pan,
Hotter than gossip at the meeting of the clan.
Geothermal giggles, erupting with flair,
Who thought the Earth had a sense of fair?

Dazzling Echoes

Echoes of laughter bounce off the walls,
A galaxy party where no one recalls.
The sound waves are wiggly, all out of sync,
Playing tag with shadows, just look and don't blink.

A comet zips by with a wink and a cheer,
Shouting, "Catch me if you can, I'm outta here!"
While stardust plays tricks and makes funny shapes,
The universe giggles, with no escapes.

Mirage of the Glowing Orb

In the sky, a yellow ball,
It whispers jokes, it makes us haul.
Tanning ducks in the bright sun's glow,
While squirrels dance, putting on a show.

It tickles noses, makes pets yawn,
In its brilliance, we bask till dawn.
A cosmic clown, with rays that tease,
Causing giggles in the summer breeze.

Searing Kisses from Above

A chubby sun with a cheeky grin,
Steals my hat as I try to begin.
Hotter than a chili's wildest dream,
Melting ice-cream, oh how it beams!

It's like a kiss, but way too hot,
With stinging rays that tie me in knots.
Chasing shadows that try to escape,
This golden gob is my sunburned mate.

The Dance of Ember and Air

A waltz of warmth with a cheeky steed,
Twirling clouds in a fiery speed.
With every prance, it grins and flares,
Cooking eggs, while folks pull chairs.

Dancing daisies with sun-kissed hues,
Under the spotlight, the grass imbues.
As the sky swirls, we giggle and sway,
On this sunny stage, let's laugh and play.

Celestial Ribbons of Warmth

Ribbons of light, a silly race,
Tickling skies with a sunburnt face.
Waving softly, it gives a nudge,
While squirrels giggle, they simply judge.

In its embrace, we wiggle around,
Where laughter and heat are joyfully found.
A cosmic jest that warms the soul,
In this bright world, let's lose control!

Sunlight's Whispers

Baking bread under the noon glow,
A butterball ball of yellow show.
Squirrels wear shades, so suave and cool,
While ants play chess on the sunny stool.

Giggles erupt from the flower beds,
With dandelions wearing tiny threads.
A bee in a tux, buzzing with flair,
Conducts a symphony in fragrant air.

Radiant Reverie

The sun sings songs of bright delight,
As squirrels strut in their disco light.
A cat in sunglasses lies on the lawn,
Winking at clouds that come and are gone.

The daisies dance, twirling a jig,
While shadows stretch, feeling quite big.
In hats atop their leafy dreams,
They laugh at life in golden beams.

Dance of the Celestial Flames

Fireflies flicker like tiny stars,
While frogs on lily pads boast of their cars.
Sunscreen slathered on all that's pale,
As humans pretend to make a sail.

Hot dogs grill while the sun takes a dive,
And clouds play tag, oh how they thrive!
A chicken in shades clucks with cheer,
While kids run amok, yelling 'No fear!'

Eclipsed Dreams

Under a blanket of shifting shade,
Imaginations dance, unafraid.
Chasing sunbeams, they skip and glide,
With shadowy friends, they laugh and hide.

The frisbee flies into a pie,
And a moment's pause gets a stifled sigh.
Mismatched socks and ice cream curls,
In the epic race of light and swirls.

The Emissary of Warmth

A ball of fire in the sky,
With shades of orange, oh my!
Spreading sizzling rays so bold,
Making ice cream melt, uncontrolled.

When it winks from half a cloud,
We squint and shield, it feels so proud.
It teases shades of tan and burn,
With each bright jig, it makes us yearn.

Celestial Gleamings

Up above, the sparkles play,
Flickering like a dance ballet.
Every twinkle, a silly wink,
Makes us pause and really think.

Glorious hues, a riotous show,
Hues of yellow, pink, and glow.
The sun's a joker, full of cheer,
With jokes to tickle, year by year.

Touches of the Incandescent Celestial

Poke at me with gentle light,
Remind me it's a sunny night.
With hands so warm, it plays a prank,
Leaves us wishing, fill up the tank!

It tickles noses, warms the toes,
And giggles softly, then it glows.
Each ray a brush, a painter's flair,
Creating giggles, everywhere!

The Kindling of Light's Touch

When beams of joy come out to play,
We laugh and dance, hip-hip-hooray!
A jester in the azure dome,
Turns our day into a joyful poem.

Chasing shadows, making hums,
Lightheartedly, it sings and drums.
With each bright burst, it shows its face,
Making life feel like a sunny race.

Flare of the Infinite

A star went out for a walk one night,
Wore shades so bright it was quite a sight.
He slipped on a comet, did a quick twirl,
And danced with the moon, giving it a whirl.

The planets all laughed, they rolled on the floor,
As he tried to impress, but fell out the door.
With a wink and a nod, he called it a day,
"Next time," he said, "I'll wear shoes on my way!"

The Brilliance of Dawn

In the morning sky, a rooster sings bright,
But it's really the sun, giving him a fright.
He thought he was grand, but the sun giggled back,
"Caw-caw, little friend, you're missing the knack!"

The clouds started puffing, like pillows of fluff,
While the sun chased their shadows, it wasn't too tough.
"Catch me if you can!" yelled the rays of gold,
But the clouds rolled their eyes, "We've seen it too bold!"

Ignite the Universe

A spark from the sun said, "Let's light the night!"
So he called up the stars, said, "Let's start this fight!"
They gathered in clusters, a comedy show,
Cracking up laughter, putting on a glow.

The black hole acted out, he stole the spotlight,
Sucking stuff in, just to cause some fright.
"Hey, don't take it all!" the bright stars exclaimed,
But the black hole just chuckled, "I'm just overamed!"

Celestial Embrace

In the whimsy of space, where giggles align,
The moon made a joke, and Venus just shined.
They cooked up a plan for a starry parade,
With comets and meteors, all ready to trade.

But the sun turned a corner, wearing a grin,
He photobombed quick, just to join in.
"Why so serious?" he yelled in delight,
"Let's laugh with the cosmos, it's out of sight!"

The Brilliant Horizon

A sunbeam slipped on a banana peel,
It winked, surprised at its own zeal.
Clouds giggled, they danced all around,
On this bright stage, laughter's the sound.

The rays wore sunglasses, feeling so cool,
While birds played games, breaking the rule.
Chasing the shadows, they played tag and spun,
Oh, what a sight—how they bask in the fun!

Echoes of the Brilliant Star

In the night sky, a star slipped and tripped,
It tumbled and rolled, giggles just chipped.
The moon made a face, couldn't quite cope,
While comets laughed loud, borrowing hope.

Far away planets threw a disco ball,
Each twinkle a wink, each shimmer a call.
Space was a party, wild and bizarre,
As everyone danced, oh, under that star!

Tidal Waves of Light

The waves of brightness crashed on the shore,
With laughter they echoed, wanting some more.
Seagulls were surfing, oh what a sight,
Dancing on beams of delightful light.

Ocean bubbles popped, each burst a cheer,
Sandy toes giggled, feeling no fear.
Look at that shimmer, a wink to the sky,
Where waves met the sun, oh my, oh my!

Illuminated Reflections

In puddles of sunlight, smiles took a dive,
Each droplet a dancer, feeling alive.
Laughter bounced back from the shiny ground,
What joy in these reflections, so wonderfully found!

Mirror-like giggles, they shimmered and glowed,
Tickling the toes of all who strode.
With every small ripple, a jest to unfold,
In this bright world, laughter turns gold!

The Firestorm of the Day

A flaring chef in a kitchen hot,
Juggles flaming pans, oh what a plot!
An omelet here, a fireball there,
Burning breakfast? Well, who would care?

The toaster pops with a joyful cheer,
Sizzling crumbs flying everywhere!
Coffee's brewing with a fragrant dance,
In this chaotic morning romance!

Shimmering Echoes in the Ether

A disco ball spins, glitter in flight,
Dancing shadows giggle, what a sight!
The cat joins in with a twist and a twirl,
While the dog just barks, giving it a whirl!

Echoes of laughter bounce off the walls,
As everyone tries not to trip and fall.
Invisible friends join the wild spree,
Painting the air with glee, you see!

Flickering Dreamscapes of Light

Fireflies giggle in the warm night breeze,
Telling jokes to the swaying trees.
They light up the path with a glowing grin,
Inviting you over to join in the din!

A wobbly moon takes a dive and rolls,
Laughing as starlight tickles our souls.
Dreams flicker on like a TV screen,
In this jumbled landscape, nothing's routine!

Luminous Whirlwinds

A whirlwind dances with a silly flair,
Pulling hats, tickling noses, it's quite a scare!
But laughter erupts as it spins on by,
Collecting giggles and butterflies shy.

Twisting and turning, the chaos is bright,
As laughter escapes into the soft night.
A rainbow of chuckles in every swirl,
In the hopping, popping, luminous whirl!

Flickers Beneath the Atmosphere

A sunbeam sneezes, oh what a sight,
It tickles the clouds, a brief delight.
Dancing shadows wear a golden hat,
While sunburned squirrels have a chat.

The horizon giggles, a bright parade,
Where sun-kissed daffodils make their trade.
A glimmer of laughter in every ray,
As it slips on a banana peel, hooray!

Bees buzzing disco, in garden lanes,
Chasing the sun like it's got no chains.
With shades on their eyes, they zoom and whirl,
In the sassy glow, they laugh and twirl.

So let's toast to rays, that flicker and flare,
With popcorn kernels in the summer air.
We'll dance to their rhythm, forever and more,
And light up our lives like never before.

The Gilded Mirage

Once upon a shimmer, a tale unfolds,
Of a mirror ball that sparkles like gold.
Reflecting giggles in the midday sun,
Where sunlit pigeons run just for fun.

Pies in the sky, how they tumble down,
With whipped cream clouds, oh what a crown!
Hats on the llamas, strutting their stuff,
As the pastry stars play, they can't get enough.

Sunflowers gossip with butterflies bright,
In this whimsical world, all feels just right.
Jumps of joy from the tulip parade,
As they waltz with the wind, a curious charade.

So follow the mirage, let giggles ignite,
In a dance with the sun, everything feels light.
We'll laugh at the trivial, embrace the bizarre,
As the gilded day ends, we still see the star.

Radiant Heartbeats

When morning beams, it casts silly spells,
Making pancakes dance, oh how they swell!
A jolly old toaster pops up with cheer,
Yelling, 'Breakfast is here, never fear!'

The sun plays hopscotch on rooftops so high,
While giggling daisies reach for the sky.
Chasing stray shadows, they spin and shout,
Letting joy overflow as they blink about.

Glowing pinatas where candy confides,
In heartbeats of laughter that tickle and glide.
So let's sing to the sun, with a fun little beat,
As the rhythm of joy makes our hearts skip a seat.

With each radiant flicker, the day will bestow,
Some mischievous magic in its golden glow.
And as night unfolds, we'll still reflect,
On whimsical warmth and the joy that we've decked.

Dance of Embered Reflections

In a puddle of light, strange critters prance,
Bouncing around in a gleeful dance.
With shadows as partners, they leap and glide,
As laughter ripples, and no one can hide.

The sun spills its tea, what a playful sight,
Painting cheeky winks, and whispers so bright.
Caterpillars join in, wearing party hats,
While the trees shake their branches, as if they're cool cats.

Twinkling ladybugs hover and play,
Making mischief in a magical way.
With a flick of their wings, they dally and sway,
In a cozy warm nook, where dreams come to stay.

So let's join the glow, it's a grand cavalcade,
Where laughter is sunny, and worries just fade.
With embered reflections that dance on our skin,
We'll treasure this moment, let the fun begin!

The Flickering Mirage

In the sky, a wink of light,
Dancing arrows, oh what a sight!
Jumping shadows, off they go,
Chasing dreams, moving slow.

Tickle me, a sunbeam's tease,
Wiggling like a slimy cheese.
Laughter echoes, bright and clear,
As we chase the rays of cheer.

A glowing frisbee, no doubt,
I'll catch it, then it'll pout!
Golden giggles, what a race,
A twinkling grin upon my face.

As the dusk begins to sway,
I laugh at light that won't stay!
Flickering mirth on the ground,
In this fun, joy is found.

A Glimpse Behind the Glare

Peek-a-boo from shining skies,
Laughter sparks as sunlight flies.
Round the corner, light does prance,
In a silly, glowy dance.

I squint and blink, what's that glow?
Funky creatures stealing the show!
With silly hats and dancing shoes,
They play in light, a raucous fuse.

Chasing shadows, flip-flop style,
Joey's now a sunlit smile.
Wobbling about like a jelly bean,
Join the frolic, bright and keen!

In the thrill of vibrant rays,
We laugh and turn this into plays.
Glimpses boisterous, pure delight,
Behind the glow, we dance in light.

Radiance in the Twilight

Here comes dusk with a bright grin,
A glow so vivid, let's all spin!
With sparkles popping, here and there,
It's a glow-fest; come and share!

Lollipops in the sunlight's glow,
We'll twirl and giggle, go with the flow.
Bouncing off walls, we're in a spree,
As luminous pranks float wild and free.

Oh, the shadows start to prance,
Wiggle those feet, it's twilight dance!
We all giggle at the bright mirage,
Chasing reflections like a collage.

In this radiant end of day,
What a playful, funny ballet!
With light at play, the twilight sings,
In the glow, we're all weird kings!

Waves of Luminous Energy

Surfing on a beam of light,
Riding waves both high and bright.
Giggles splash as we glide along,
To this silly, shining song.

Jumping over radiant swells,
Whacky tales that laughter tells.
With every toss, we twist and shout,
This glowing game, no doubt, no doubt!

Wipes of glow across our face,
In this goofy, shining race.
A bright burst makes us all squeal,
What's this? Just a glowing wheel!

So come aboard, let's ride the light,
With radiant energy, we take flight.
In waves of giggles and a swirl,
We're the kings of this glowing whirl!

Radiance Unbound

In a cosmic dance, we prance around,
With shades of yellow, humor is found.
Stars tickle the sky, like a joke gone wild,
While space laughs softly, like a cheerful child.

Galaxies twirl in a playful embrace,
While comets dash by, just for the chase.
Celestial bodies in a comedy show,
As meteors wink with a twinkling glow.

Planets in line, in an awkward wait,
Like they're all queuing up for a date.
Yet each puff of gas, just floats away,
Saying, "Catch me if you can!" in a cosmic play.

So let's toast to the laughter up high,
To the wonders of space that can't say goodbye.
For joy in the stars is the ultimate quest,
With giggles and grins, we're truly blessed.

Flames of the Distant Star

A fiery friend in the night sky beams,
With puns so hot, it's bursting with dreams.
Winking down at us, it knows it's a star,
Making sure laughter travels far.

Dancing in orbit, it's quite the tease,
With solar tickles that aim to please.
Bouncing around like a cosmic clown,
While sunbeams giggle, lighting the town.

Comets tail behind with a flick and a grin,
As if playing tag, they're eager to win.
With each burst of light, a chuckle ignites,
Cause even in space, we enjoy silly nights.

So raise your glass to the flames that delight,
In a universe where jokes ignite.
For in every gleam, there's a secret to see,
A laughter-filled cosmos, just you and me.

Dawn Breaks with Fire

As day breaks anew with a fiery glow,
The sun yawns wide, putting on quite a show.
Rays stretch and giggle, painting the skies,
With hues of orange that tickle the eyes.

Birds chirp with joy, they can't help but cheer,
For the dawn's warm embrace, so inviting and near.
A fresh cup of coffee warms up the soul,
While sunlight jests, "Hey, let's rock and roll!"

Morning shadows dance, in a game of hide,
As laughter tumbles down the hillside.
The warmth wraps us up, like a cozy old friend,
Promising joy as the daylight ascends.

So step into this day, let the fun be your guide,
With the sun's silly spark, take it all in stride.
For in every sunrise, there's a giggle to find,
With laughter as light as a gentle wind's bind.

Unseen Currents of Warmth

Invisible waves in the air we breathe,
Whispering chuckles that wrap and weave.
A gentle touch, like a friend's embrace,
Tickling our senses with joy and grace.

Breezes conspire with a mischievous grin,
As they flutter our hair and pull us within.
The sun hides beneath, just playing coy,
Casting a warmth that brings endless joy.

Heat from above, a secret delight,
Makes us dance silly from morning till night.
With each passing gust, let out a giggle,
For warmth in the air makes our hearts wiggle.

So laugh with the currents, let worries unfold,
The unseen joy that the universe holds.
For in every breeze, there's a jest waiting there,
Whispering, "Join in, come share the affair!"

The Fiery Auras of Space

In the vast dark night, a dance begins,
A cosmic jest, where laughter spins.
Stars wearing shades, all cool and bright,
Tickling planets in the quiet of night.

Comets with wigs, they swirl and twirl,
Making the galaxies giggle and whirl.
Asteroids playing tag, oh what a sight,
Who knew the cosmos had such delight?

Nebulas puffing up like cotton candy,
In a universe so dazzling and dandy.
Supernovas burst with a pop and a cheer,
While black holes conjure a curious leer.

Even the moons join in the fun,
Wobbling about, they dance and run.
The fiery auras chuckle with glee,
As the universe sprinkles its humor for free.

Heated Whispers of the Sky

A heated breeze brings chuckles to light,
Clouds gossip above, in the warm twilight.
The sun gives a wink, with rays like a grin,
While planets debate who's the brightest in spin.

Breezes play tricks, nudging stars in their bed,
Making them giggle, twinkling instead.
The sun does a shimmy, in shades of gold,
While the moon looks on, feeling none too old.

Meteor showers drop in for a chat,
Making jokes about a cosmic brat.
With each little sparkle, they burst into cheer,
Oh, the warmth of the sky, what a comic frontier!

Galaxies laugh in their swirling embrace,
While comets high-five, in a wild race.
Heated whispers floating, oh what a gain,
In the rosy sky, where humor is lain.

Reflections of Distant Brilliance

In the shimmering void, bright thoughts collide,
Stars reflecting giggles, like jokes worldwide.
With flashes and twinkles, they share the delight,
Echoing laughter, in the cool of the night.

Planets in hues of pink, orange, and blue,
Join in the fun, with a wink or two.
They bounce cosmic puns from one to the next,
Creating a tapestry, humorously perplexed.

Distant worlds peek from behind their veil,
Trading tales that make even comets wail.
Starlight's the messenger, giggles ignited,
In a universe vast, where whims are invited.

Across nebulas bright, the chuckles do swell,
With cosmic reflections, a whimsical spell.
Whirling and dancing, they brighten the night,
In the laughter of worlds, everything feels right.

Warm Caress of the Ether

A warm caress dances on waves of the space,
Whispers of mirth, the stars interlace.
With ticklish rays, they embrace the night,
Twirling in joy, a comical sight.

Shooting stars laugh, racing each other around,
In the delicious embrace of the cosmic sound.
Waving at planets, they wink and they sway,
In a playful ballet, oh what a display!

Suns toast their marshmallows with radiant flair,
As meteors dash, like they don't have a care.
Warmth from the ether tickles the spine,
In this cosmic corner, all humor's divine.

The asteroids chuckle, in playful pursuits,
While cosmic winds fan the flames of their roots.
In the embrace of the ether, jokes lightly soar,
As laughter's the light that we all can explore.

Incandescence in the Sky

Up above, the sun does wink,
Its rays like fingers, pink,
Birds wear shades, it's quite a sight,
As clouds get jealous, take to flight.

The shadows play a little game,
They stretch and jump, oh what a name!
A silly dance on sunny ground,
Where laughter echoes all around.

The trees all nod, their leaves in glee,
As squirrels flip in harmony.
With every beam, they crack a joke,
The sun just grins, a friend invoked.

So let us bask, in this delight,
As nature giggles, oh so bright!
With joy and mirth upon the grass,
In this warm glow, we all have class.

Dawn's Alchemy

Morning paints the sky in gold,
With brushes made from tales of old.
The rooster crows, a bit too loud,
While sleepy heads form quite a crowd.

Bacon sizzles like the sun,
Dancing in the skillet, fun!
Toast pops up, it steals the show,
But jam just wants to spread the glow.

The cat stretches, yawns with flair,
Pretending it just doesn't care.
Meanwhile, birds throw a revue,
A chirpy tune, their morning cue.

With every ray, we crack a smile,
The dawn's weird magic, all worthwhile.
So grab your cup, let's sip away,
And laugh at life, a brand new day.

Dance of the Radiant Skies

A glowing ribbon weaves up high,
Where clouds transform and float on by.
With sunbeams prancing in a line,
It's nature's twist—oh, how divine!

The moon looks on with jealous eyes,
As sunshine sprinkles its surprise.
Daytime parties, night takes a seat,
While shadows linger, feeling beat.

Bees buzz and twirl with happy zest,
They've got moves, you wouldn't guess!
The flowers sway, a blooming cheer,
In this bright ballet, we all appear.

From dawn till dusk, what a parade,
Where laughter sings and worries fade.
So let's embrace this quirky show,
And dance beneath the radiant glow.

A Symphony of Sunbeams

The sun conducts a grand affair,
With beams that wiggle without a care.
Instruments of nature play away,
As little critters join the fray.

The lightest notes, a fluttering breeze,
As trees sway gently, like happy peas.
The flowers march in perfect rows,
And hummingbirds steal all the bows.

A silly tune of bees and blooms,
Where laughter dances in the rooms.
Each ray brings giggles, bright and bold,
In this playful world, we strike gold.

Together we sing this joyful song,
In sunlit symphonies, we belong.
With every chord, our smiles expand,
United under this radiant band.

The Canvas of Fiery Mornings

The sun wakes up and spills its tea,
A splash of orange, wild and free.
The clouds wear hues of raspberry and gold,
A canvas bright, a sight to behold.

Birds in bow ties start the show,
Chirping tunes, they steal the glow.
The trees dance along, sway side to side,
As if they're all part of this joyride.

Coffee pots hum, they join the fun,
Bubbling laughter, oh what a run!
Toast pops up like a jack in a box,
Grinning wide, it struts and rocks.

And as the day begins to unfold,
With tales and antics just waiting to be told,
We bask in the hues, the giggles, the cheer,
In this fiery morn, we forget all fear.

Fusion of Light and Life

A dance of photons spins so bright,
Running wild in the morning light.
The flowers blush, they can't resist,
A sunbeam's kiss, a generous twist.

Squirrels wear shades, strutting with flair,
Chasing their tails, without a care.
The daisies are swaying, they clap their leaves,
As laughter erupts, in nature's reprieves.

The mellow warmth, a cozy embrace,
Melts away all frowns from the face.
Even the rocks begin to cheer,
As shadows play tag, the fun is here!

In this vibrant mix, life sings aloud,
The sky wears a smile, drawn from the crowd.
Joy fizzes up like soda in a glass,
In this light, every worry will pass.

The Embrace of Day's Warmth

With open arms, the sun does greet,
Wrapping the world in a warm sheet.
The squirrels giggle, teasing the breeze,
While butterflies dance among the trees.

The cat sprawls out, soaking it in,
Dreaming of treats and mischief to begin.
The flowers wiggle, they rattle and sway,
In this glowing hug, they love to play.

Chasing shadows, the children run,
Squealing with joy, oh, what fun!
The sunbeams tickle and stretch so far,
Every ray shining like a bright star.

And as day lingers, with laughter in tow,
The warmth we share continues to grow.
In every smile, we find our worth,
In the embrace of day, we dance on Earth.

Elysian Flare

In a realm where the colors ignite,
Laughter dances, oh what a sight!
The daisies chuckle with each cool breeze,
While the sun plays tricks, does as it pleases.

The rabbits hop in a silly parade,
Wearing little hats that they proudly made.
The hops are bold, the rolls are grand,
In this playful land, all hold hands.

Tickled by rays, we twirl about,
In every heart, there's no room for doubt.
The skies giggle as clouds fluff and tease,
This merry realm puts us all at ease.

With every moment, we unleash our flair,
Filling the air with joy we share.
In this fusion of fun, we take our stand,
In the elysium of sun-kissed land.

Gale of Golden Rays

A sunbeam slipped on a banana peel,
It rolled and tumbled, oh what a reel!
Chasing shadows in a silly chase,
While clouds above giggle in their space.

The light decided to play peek-a-boo,
Tickling noses with its bright hue.
"Catch me if you can," the sun did proclaim,
But the trees just waved, without any shame.

The squirrels danced, doing their best jig,
Under the sun, feeling quite big.
With rays of laughter splashing about,
Even grumpy old cats couldn't pout.

So let's frolic in this golden bliss,
With beams of joy we cannot miss.
Nature's stage glimmers in delight,
As daylight sparkles, oh what a sight!

The Dance of Celestial Flames

Flames in the sky started to prance,
Stars joined in for a twinkling dance.
The moon pulled a muscle, then laughed so wide,
Wobbling around in its silvery stride.

Planets rolled their eyes, in a playful mood,
As comets zipped by, all shiny and crude.
"You call that a spin?" laughed the gold star bright,
"Try a cartwheel, come join the delight!"

The sun wore shades to shield its gaze,
While shooting stars gave out free razzle-dazzle praise.
Asteroids bounced, having a grand ball,
With cosmic confetti, they decorated all.

In this hilarious orchestra of lights,
Each wink and blink ignites the nights.
So grab a buddy, let's boogie and sway,
With laughter echoing through the Milky Way!

Veils of Photonic Wonders

Waves of colors swirling in the air,
Painted rainbows that tickle with flair.
Light beams caught in a delicate spin,
Glittering giggles where the fun begins.

The sun wore a hat, quite floppy and bright,
Turned to the moon, said, "What a sight!"
The moon chuckled softly, "Let's share a grin,
In this wild theater, let the fun begin!"

They played a game of who can glow more,
As the garden critters began to explore.
Fireflies buzzed, turning on their lights,
In a sparkling party that lasted all nights.

Spectacular shapes in a playful show,
A dance of photons that steals the glow.
Everyone joined in, from young to old,
Laughing, they twinkled in hues of gold!

Rippled Light on Water

Waves giggled softly, splashing around,
Light played tag with the fish underground.
The sun peeked down with a cheeky grin,
"Hope you all catch those beams of fun!"

Reflections danced like silly ducks,
While water sprites chuckled, "What luck!"
Boat paddles splashed, creating a whirl,
And the frogs croaked, spinning in a twirl.

Every ripple sparkled with laughter anew,
As ducks waddled by, in a row of two.
The breeze joined in with a whimsical song,
And nature sang along, where we all belong.

So let us bask in this watery spree,
Where giggles and glimmers are wild and free.
Join the shenanigans, come take a seat,
As rippled light dances to a joyful beat!

Flames of Distant Worlds

Across the sky, a prankster glows,
It tickles planets with bright elbows.
Bringing warmth to each comical dance,
While stars giggle in their cosmic pants.

The moon said, "Hey, don't get too close!"
As comets fly by with a cheeky boast.
A cosmic party, where no one's shy,
Each solar flare is a pie in the sky!

Jokes are traded in beams of light,
Planets chuckle, all day and night.
Even black holes can't swallow their glee,
In this universe of hilarity!

So here's to sparks that tickle and tease,
Distant worlds swaying like they're at ease.
Let laughter reign in celestial space,
While our star throws a whimsical race!

Horizon's Fever Dream

Out on the edge, where the wild winds howl,
The sun starts to giggle, like a happy owl.
Golden rays burst forth with a twist,
Creating shadows that dance and twist!

Clouds turn into marshmallows, oh so sweet,
While sunbeams tap-dance on the ground with their feet.
Daydreams flicker in a bright ballet,
As horizons stretch in a silly display!

Watch out for the sun with its playful spark,
Drawing chalk lines up high in the dark.
It's a fever dream of comic delight,
Where every sunset's a joke in the night!

So let's toast to sunsets, both rosy and red,
For laughs we share, as light paints the spread.
In this fever dream, we find our rhyme,
And dance with the sun, till the end of time!

The Sun's Gentle Hand

With a wink and a smile, the day begins,
The sun's gentle hand pulls us from our sins.
It whispers jokes that float on warm air,
While shadows laugh without a single care.

Sunscreen smiles on our nose like a clown,
As UV rays play tag in the town.
"It's a hot one!" the ice cream truck sings,
While we chase after sweet, melting things!

Bouncing beams ricochet off trees,
Tickling our toes in a light summer breeze.
Kick off your shoes, join the sun's parade,
As laughter bounces in the light's cascade!

So here's to the sun, with its playful charm,
Keeping us cheerful and safe from harm.
With each gentle touch, it spreads joy and cheer,
Turning our worries to bright, sunny clear!

Luminous Threads of Time

Woven in light, the days spin on by,
Threading laughter through the big, starry sky.
Moments flaring like popcorn in space,
Making history dance at a lightning pace!

Tick-tock goes the clock, but who cares for time?
When cosmic cheer leads our hearts to rhyme.
Stars giggle softly at events gone awry,
While constellations wink with a twinkling eye!

Past and future merge in a sparkly swirl,
As galaxies giggle, spinning and twirl.
Each twist in the thread a joke in disguise,
Beneath the glow of a billion bright eyes!

So let's raise a toast, to the jesters of fate,
For in this grand web, we all share a plate.
With luminous threads, we weave our own song,
In this cosmic comedy, where we all belong!

Elysium of Ember

In a land where sunbeams dance,
The fireflies wear their best pants.
With laughter loud as a sunbeam's sway,
We chase our shadows all day.

The butterflies sip their fruity drinks,
While chatting about the sun's bright winks.
We roast marshmallows under the glow,
And giggle at clouds that put on a show.

A squirrel juggles nuts with flair,
While flamingos strut without a care.
In this realm of warmth and play,
Every moment shines like a cabaret.

As night drapes in its velvet cape,
We trade our tales, every shape.
With giggles that tickle the starlit air,
In this embered joy, we have no despair.

Starlit Dawn

When the dawn breaks with a wink,
The roosters sing, and the rabbits drink.
Pancakes flip in perfect arcs,
While the squirrel performs his morning larks.

Sunbeams skate on grassy plains,
Ticklish breezes pull at our lanes.
We bounce like balls under the haze,
In the light of joyous rays.

The daisies dance in the morning dew,
As we giggle and skip in a funner hue.
The frogs join in with a ribbiting cheer,
Celebrating dawn, our favorite time of year.

With each tickle from the sun above,
We scatter giggles like fit-for-love.
In this starlit magic, wild and free,
Our laughter rings out, just like a melody.

Chromatic Horizons

Painting the sky with shades of cheer,
Colors collide, oh so near!
Marigolds tickle the daisies' toes,
While we line up in funny rows.

The horizon wears its brightest cheer,
As clouds march by, we point and jeer.
Silly hats on every face,
In this riot of hues, we find our place.

With crayons bright, we live and play,
Drawing sunbeams that twist and sway.
Jumping through rainbows like sprightly gnomes,
Singing silly songs from our colorful homes.

Each shade a story, a giggle or two,
As we dance in glee in our grand debut.
At the edge of the world, where laughter resides,
In chromatic realms, our joy collides.

A Tapestry of Radiance

In a land where laughter's spun,
Every thread gleams, oh what fun!
We weave our jokes with golden rays,
Creating smiles for countless days.

Mirthful mimosas fill the air,
While a puppy prances without a care.
Knitting joy with each cackle and roar,
This tapestry holds hearts galore.

The sun's a jester, flipping around,
Tickling flowers, spreading sound.
With each stitch, we plant our flair,
In this radiant quilt, giggles declare.

As twilight wraps our playful spree,
We bask in happiness, wild and free.
With stars now woven in our embrace,
In this radiant fabric, we find our place.

The Brilliance of Daybreak

A rooster crows, it's time to rise,
But I just want to close my eyes.
The sun peeks in, a cheeky grin,
   Laughing at my sleepy skin.

Coffee brews, a fragrant dance,
I spill it twice, oh what a chance!
The birds chirp jokes in harmony,
   As I trip over my own two feet.

The sky's a canvas, yellow and pink,
I think I'm awake, but still need a drink.
A squirrel steals my muffin, the nerve!
As I wave goodbye to my breakfast swerve.

Sunshine sprinkles, like confetti rain,
   Chasing away my nighttime pain.
With laughter echoing through the trees,
   Daylight dances on a sneezy breeze.

Whispers of the Sunlit Sphere

Bright rays giggle, oh so bright,
Tickling my face with pure delight.
A butterfly winks and flits on by,
"Catch me if you can!" it dares, oh my!

I wear my shades to look real cool,
But trip on grass, oh what a fool!
The sun winks down, "Don't take it slow,"
As I pretend it's just part of the show.

Clouds gather round, like a cozy gang,
Making shadows, and oh, how they sang!
"Let's play hide and seek," they say with glee,
But finding the sun? A mystery for me!

As evening draws, it takes a bow,
With a red-orange hue, I've got to wow.
The stars peek out, giggling all night,
"Good luck, dear sun, till tomorrow's light!"

An Odyssey of Light and Heat

The sun's on a mission, bright and spry,
Chasing clouds, oh my, oh my!
It tickles the rooftops, bathes the grass,
But I'm just trying to get off my… class.

Bees buzz around like old-time jazz,
Sipping nectar, giving me pizzazz.
I try to dance but twist my shoe,
The sun laughs down, "Hey, me too!"

A picnic planned, all set to feast,
But ants are there, multiplying like yeast.
The sunlight glistens on sandwich bread,
Along with the crumbs that danced and fled!

As we retreat from the sizzling day,
The sun waves goodbye in a silly way.
With laughter echoing in the fading light,
I tip my hat, what a funny sight!

The Fervid Embrace

The sun hugs tightly, like mom at noon,
   Sweaty hugs, oh, who needs a tune?
   I twirl and fling with fingers fanned,
    But to the shade, my feet command!

    Waves of warmth, a playful tease,
Sunburns whisper, "You can't appease!"
   I slather on lotion, a slippery mess,
    "Why me, dear sun?" I must confess.

    Colors of summer, bright and bold,
   Melons and laughter, stories retold.
  The sun must giggle as we all get red,
  With lemonade flowing, cheers ahead!

  As night creeps in, the heat does fade,
    I recall the day in a silly parade.
   The sun will return, no need to beg,
For another round of warmth and egg!

Sunlit Reveries

A sunbeam dances on my nose,
It tickles me, and then it glows.
I sneeze and ducks all take to flight,
They think it's me that's full of light.

In summer's warmth, we start to sweat,
With ice cream cones, it's hard to fret.
The sun's a joker, plays his part,
Turns us into sunburnt art.

Corn on the cob, it pops and sizzles,
The sun's up high, it laughs and giggles.
We chase the rays, we chase the fun,
Yet burn our buns—oh how we run!

When the sun dips low, we play our tunes,
Dancing shadows, like cheeky raccoons.
It's a sunny joke, with lots of cheer,
Just don't forget your sunscreen, dear!

Pulses of the Sun's Heart

The sun woke up and bumped its head,
It stretched so wide, then hats it shed.
With rays that bounce and skip away,
It's like a kid who's lost at play.

A sun hat flies across the park,
That squirrel's now wearing it—oh hark!
The heatwaves wobble, bend, and sway,
Sunshine slacklines on a bright display.

We juggle lemonade and lime,
The sun throws parties, every time.
With palm trees dancing in a line,
It's hard to tell just who steals shine!

As evenings end, we gather round,
With the sun's pulse, we laugh and bound.
A burst of laughter fills the air,
Even as we flop—sun's still there!

Flashes in the Aurora's Veil

There's a cosmic dance, oh what a show,
With colors bright that twirl and flow.
The moon's a spy, with knick-knack laughs,
As stars perform their goofy gaffs.

The lights are playful, going mad,
Dancing fries that make you glad.
With giggles high and chuckles bold,
The sky concocts a tale retold.

From green to pink, what a display,
A playful wisp, that leads the way.
We wear our shades to watch the glow,
Join in the fun, let laughter flow!

As night rolls in with dreamy grace,
The stars join in, to join the race.
With every twinkle, every flare,
They tell us jokes, oh, how we stare!

Illuminated Echoes

When daylight dips like a sweet refrain,
The sun's a prankster, can't contain.
It winks at us with cheeky flair,
And whispers secrets, everywhere.

We dance amongst the twilight beams,
Creating shadows, fueling dreams.
With giggles shared and echoing, too,
The sun's last laugh—just me and you!

Balloons float high, catching the gleam,
As stars come out to join our team.
We laugh so hard, we lose our breath,
With life so bright, who needs to rest?

The night encroaches, but what a thrill,
With echoes sparkling, hearts to fill.
The sun may sleep, but here we stay,
In laughter's light, we'll find our way!

Tender Caresses of Heat

The sun is a great big ball of fun,
Tickling clouds while everyone runs.
Its rays are sharp like a playful knife,
Chasing away the nappers' strife.

Sunscreen battles, slap, slap, slap,
Sizzling on sand, it's a sticky trap.
We fry our burgers and our toes too,
But eating hot dogs? That's too askew!

The sun's a comedian, don't you see?
Dancing around with glee and gaffs, you agree?
But if it gets too bright, oh dear, don't fret,
Just wear shades and don't break a sweat!

As evening blooms, we breathe a sigh,
That hot fluorescent lamp in the sky.
With colors melting, laughter so bold,
Come on, silly sun, let's watch stories unfold!

Trails of the Sun's Embrace

Bouncing on beams like a silly rabbit,
The sun's warm glow—oh, what a habit!
While shadows play tricks, the giggles ignite,
With each step of warmth, the world feels right!

Picnics on grass become a great quest,
Ants join the feast; they're our tiny guests.
A sun tea party, we brew with cheer,
Steeped in sunshine and laughter so dear!

Beach balls are flying, a colorful sight,
Water balloons ready, oh what a delight!
But watch for the splash from the mischievous friend,
Giggles galore as the fun won't end!

As sunsets remind us to wind down the play,
The glow of the horizon steals night from the day.
With moonlit memories, frighteningly grand,
Tomorrow we'll sunbathe in this infinite land!

Celestial Sparks

Galactic giggles twinkle in the night,
Stars tease the moon; oh what a sight!
When comets zoom by, they wink and dance,
As if they're ignoring their cosmic chance!

Shooting stars make wishes with a twist,
But what if they trip? Oh, you get the gist!
They tumble like clowns, such slapstick fun,
While cosmic dust sprouts a bright running sun.

The universe chuckles, can't hold its breath,
Sending bubbles of joy that feel like a fest.
Neon galaxies swirl in a party of light,
And every glittering gem is a joke in flight!

So let's join this jest, with ecstasy found,
With laughter like laughter, that's cosmic, profound.
Embrace your starlight, let humor unfurl,
For in this vast universe, we twirl and we twirl!

Illumination for the Lost

When the day's play ends, the seekers arise,
With flashlights in hand and twinkles in eyes.
"Where's the path?" they cheerfully yell,
As shadows play tricks, oh, can't you tell?

They wander through parks with laughter so free,
But every wrong turn feels like a spree.
A firefly's flicker, a guiding torch,
Yet they still can't find where they left the porch!

A map made of giggles unfolds in the air,
With stars as our guides, we'll laugh without care.
"Who needs a plan when we have our fun?
If we get lost, we'll still shine like the sun!"

So here's to the wanderers, oh so bold,
In the night's gentle grip, they find their gold.
With laughter as lanterns, confusion in tow,
In the light of the giggles, off we go!

The Luminous Surge

The sun burst forth with a cheeky grin,
Danced with delight as it began to spin.
Sunbeams twirled, like they lost their way,
Winking at shadows, they laughed in play.

Bright rays were bouncing, oh what a show,
Lighting up puddles, making them glow.
Everyone squinted, shielding their eyes,
While squirrels in shades plotted their surprise.

Birds in a frenzy, on beams they soared,
Chirping like crazy, never bored.
"Look at us," they said with flair,
"Sunshine's the reason we're all up in the air!"

With sparks and giggles, the day rolled on,
The mascot of laughter, that glowing dawn.
In a world brimming with light so absurd,
Who knew a bright day could be so disturbed!

Blazing Wings of Dawn

A rooster cried out, but forgot the tune,
He joined in the dance with the morning moon.
Dawn rolled in like a jovial jester,
Waving goodbye to the sleepy investor.

With wings that shimmered, the bugs took flight,
Wobbling around in pure delight.
"Is this a circus or morning's embrace?"
They tangled in laughter, a light-hearted race.

The flowers filed in, all dressed in sun,
Strutting their petals, just having fun.
A bee on a mission buzzed all around,
Mistaking the tulip for a lively clown.

As sunlight tickled the grassy bed,
The world laughed along, no worries to dread.
With every giggle that came from the dawn,
Nature was sure, it was the time to fawn!

Threads of Light in the Atmosphere

Woven like laughter, the sky spun bright,
With threads of warmth, they danced in flight.
Clouds got frisky, spinning in glee,
Whispering secrets of joy 'neath the tree.

The sun tossed confetti, in colors so bold,
While the moon tried to tell tales of old.
"Can we party with stars?" the sun seemed to say,
So they all hopped around, in their dazzling display.

The breeze chimed in, playing a tune,
Making leaves jiggle, like folks at noon.
"Bring on the giggles, let's give it a whirl,
Watch us all twinkle, and spin in a swirl!"

With rays of laughter threading through air,
The sky hosted parties—beyond compare.
As day turned to night, under glittered skies,
The world twinkled back, with amusing surprise!

The Brilliant Tempest

Oh, the tempest arrived with a comical twist,
Lightning did jiggles, too wild to resist.
Clouds rolled in grumpy, but lightened their mood,
Once they saw raindrops dressed up in food!

The thunder giggled, it rumbled and laughed,
As the wind joined the tune, becoming quite daft.
"Let's shower the ground with some silly old tunes,
Maybe a snippet of toddlerty cartoons!"

Puddles became stages for frogs and their gang,
They croaked their best hits, as if they were fang.
Each drop was a note, each flash was a dance,
In the zany tempest, all creatures took a chance.

As skies turned to dark, the giggles grew loud,
The storm had become quite the whimsical crowd.
With laughter and rumbles, they played till the end,
Who knew a tempest could be the best friend?

Horizon's Golden Kiss

As dawn peeks in with a grin,
The roosters dance, let the fun begin!
Coffee spills, I trip on my shoe,
The sun laughs loud—it's up to its cue.

Pancakes flip in a sunbeam's glow,
Butter slides like it's on a show.
A sticky jam of morning delight,
The horizon winks, what a silly sight!

Birds chirp tunes of morning glee,
A cat's caught napping—oh, what a spree!
The golden kisses sparkle and shine,
As laughter twirls in the breakfast line.

Oh, morning sun, you cheeky tease,
With warm embraces that surely please.
As I dash out, I trip once more,
Horizon, you've won! I'll call it a score.

A Symphony of Light

A beam spills notes on rooftops high,
The shadows dance, under the sky.
Trombones blare, and trumpets swoon,
As sunlit tunes play afternoon.

Squirrels join with their acorn flutes,
While bushes sway in silly boots.
The sun raises its baton with flair,
Conducting giggles that fill the air.

Dancing daisies in a grand parade,
Each petal sways, though slightly frayed.
With every beam, a chuckle's shared,
In this light show, no one's prepared!

Laughter echoes through the trees,
As critters join the sunlit tease.
What a symphony of joyful sights,
With silly smiles that the sun ignites!

The Sun's Luminous Heart

In the sky, a joker's big laugh,
The sun beams wide—what a photograph!
It tickles clouds, a fluffy friend,
With rays that swirl and twist, descend.

A fluffy kitten chases a beam,
Bounding forth in a playful dream.
The sun's heart beats with giggles bright,
It shines on mischief throughout the night!

It bakes the pavement, oh what a tease,
Ice creams melt under its warm ease.
We dive in pools to escape the glow,
But the radiant heart still steals the show!

Every sunset is a wink of glee,
As shadows stretch for a suntan spree.
The luminous heart beats just for fun,
A chuckle shared, we're all (solar) one!

Gilded Rays of Hope

In a field of flowers, rays jump high,
They twirl and twist, oh my, oh my!
Waking dreams on a canvas bright,
Colors burst in the morning light.

Bumbles buzz, in sun's warm embrace,
A dance together, oh what a race!
The world adorned in a golden dress,
With joyful glimmers, who could guess?

Picnics spread below the gleam,
With laughter echoing like a dream.
Each snack shared under radiant skies,
The gilded rays catch all the sighs.

So gather 'round, let the fun commence,
With memories made, it all makes sense.
In dazzling light, our spirits soar,
With gilded rays, we always want more!

www.ingramcontent.com/pod-product-compliance
Lightning Source LLC
Chambersburg PA
CBHW071845160426
43209CB00003B/415